Dear You

Ryan Banko

Presentation by *BookLeaf Publishing*

Web: www.bookleafpub.com

E-mail: info@bookleafpub.com

ISBN: 9789358369045

First edition 2023

DEDICATION

For Aaron.

I wish you could see me now and how I am growing into the person I was born to be. Someday I would very much like to lay my head down after a long day and finally feel a sense of calm that will accompany the feeling that I have made you proud. And until that day, I will not stop working tirelessly and endlessly to achieve that.

ACKNOWLEDGEMENT

I would like to acknowledge everyone I have met in my life. This includes those who have stuck around through all the messes, those who left on their own accord, those who made me smile, those who made me cry, those who made me hurt, and those of whom I have made hurt. Life is a collection of memories from events, both exciting and traumatic, and none of these pieces would be possible without any of you. Although the majority are not happy pieces, the emotions behind them are heavy and true, and none of them would exist without crossing paths with the people I have so far in this journey we call life.

PREFACE

I wrote these pieces for Dear You as a way to challenge myself for 21 straight days of writing in May of 2023. Yes, some of these are darker and emotional pieces, some I never really desired to share with the world. Yet, here we are! I felt the only way to truly invoke the emotions I felt during these life situations was to put them all out there for the world to see and feel. Some are sad, some are lost, some are confused, and some are hopeful. Dear You is a poetic letter to myself, and to you all, to not shy and run away from your emotions, but to accept them, learn from them, live with them, and grow from them. I started this project during a new found low, but ended it on a fairly high note. I am always improving my situation on the daily, despite it all. My only hope is that you all can too.

Intro

Introducing to this page
Is a person of a young age
Still finding their place
In a very crowded space
Unfortunately on this day
They did lose their way
And though it isn't yet clear
This will be everything they fear
Unsure of what all went down
They are helpless and frown
As their emotions begin to storm
The rivers of tears start to form
And as the sun begins to set
They don't know what is in store yet

This person knows not what to do.
This person has no clue.
This person surely is blue.
This person is you.

The Next Day

So you've woken up
But something feels off
An emotional buildup
Is about to blastoff.

Without a warning
Tears consume your face
There goes your morning
As your mind starts to race.

You stare at the wall
Toxic overthinking
You move down the hall
Without even blinking.

You do have a pulse
But you cannot breathe
Should've trusted your impulse
Your emotions seethe

It's only the first day
It doesn't seem like it
But it'll be okay
Although it'll take a bit.

Let's Try Some of This

You feel yourself slipping
The day doesn't end
Your heart's been ripping
You just need a friend

But no one is there
You're all alone
You pull out your hair
Seeing a silent phone

Your emotions are glum
You feel so so much
But also feel numb
You need a crutch

The crutch is a drink
You want to forget
But it makes you think
Now you only fret

You see some more glass
"Let's try some of this"
It puts you on your ass
Your day you dismiss

Drunk

When I go out and drink
I always just think
Maybe I'll get over you
But I never seem to do
Instead, I think more
And my mind gets sore
I can't get you out of my head
Even when I lay in bed
The thought of you remains
And numbness fills my veins

Through the pain I plow,
As I try to stay sober, now.

Names

I've been called Ryan, I've been called Harry,
I've been called Banko
Bankster
Banksidoodle
Bro
Buddy
Annoying
A friend
A homie
A boyfriend
A best friend
A son
A brother
A coach
A coworker
A member
A teammate
& A lover.

Of all the names I've been called, I've always
knew who they were talking to.
But when you call me by my name, I don't know
with whom you wish to speak.
When you call me by my name, I don't know
who I am.

When you call out my name, I feel more lost
than I've ever felt before.

Games

You said you weren't here to play no game
Yet you made me feel fucking lame
I told you straight up and kept it real
You couldn't even tell me what you feel
All I asked was for you to talk to me
Just tell me when you stop feelin it
So you can set me free
But you didn't give a shit

So I scream
And I yell
But you'll never know
How you put me through hell
The fact that you can hurt me:
The guy who wanted to give you the world.
And you can't even say you're sorry
I'll never be able to understand
How you could hurt me the way you did
And walk away like nothing happened
And my favorite part
Is how appalled you act
When I finally stand up for myself
And you tell the world how out of pocket it was
Yet
When all this started

I asked you to be upfront and honest
And if you weren't feeling it to let me know
So I wasn't waiting for nothing
& looking like a bum waiting for something
Something that was to never come
So thanks for that
Thanks for saying you thought I wanted to be
friends
Thanks for saying you lost interest
Thanks for saying it after the fact
Thanks for letting me die every night
Thanks for letting me fall apart
Thanks for letting me think it was me
Thanks for letting me feel the worst pain of my
life
Thanks for watching me suffer alone
Thanks for not caring
And thank you for walking away.

My Days (2016)

I spend my days
Sitting in a daze
My eyes just gaze
In the summer haze
Mind trapped in a maze
In a depress-ed phase
I start to craze
While my body stays,
My emotions part ways.
Meandering the bays
I'm seeking praise
My life-a group of tragic plays…

I Am Who I AM

I opened myself to you
You saw inside where others don't
You made me comfortable
You made me safe
You made me laugh
I enjoyed so much that feeling
I am grateful.

Then you made me cry.
You shut me out
You lifted me up,
Just to drop me down
From the highest of highs
To the lowest of lows
Who I was wasn't good enough
Not to keep around
Whether to help
Whether to hug
Whether to hold
You left me broken
Parts of me died when it all went bad.
Parts of me I was polishing up,
Parts of me that would've given you the world,
Parts of me that would've done anything for
you,

Parts of me that saw the beauty in your crazy.
But that's all gone now
I wish it wasn't, but it is.
You left me lost in an abyss.

But,
At the end of the day
I'll look in the mirror
Though my thoughts are gray
I still see me
Today is a little clearer
No, not yet happy
But still
I Am Who I Am
And that's a beautiful thing.

Maybe Someday

I hope that Maybe Someday
Somewhere along the way
That we Can just talk
Maybe even go for a walk
Start off with just a "hey"

Maybe Someday
We can go sit at a park
Talk about what went wrong
Then listen to our song
We can stay till it's dark

Maybe Someday
We can talk without a fight
We can listen and understand
And hold each other in the sand
As we sit on the beach at night

Maybe Someday
I'll look you in your eyes
And tell you I'm sorry
And on that night, so starry
Maybe then, my sorrow dies

Wide Awake

Little did you know
While you went to sleep
I was wide awake
Tossing
Turning
Restless.
The hurt I was feeling

While you were fast asleep
The one you hurt the most
The one that cared for you
They suffered in silence
Alone.
Alone in the dark
Tears obscuring their face
Trembles consuming their body
Pain
Pain beyond any physical toll they knew
Oh how their heart fell wretched from their chest
Pulled out and present to you
Everything they had there for you
You took a good look at it
And without a word or hesitation
You simple walked away
Leaving them stranded

Once more alone
With heart in their hand
On their knees
Going from giving everything
To ready to give up
And yet you wonder why they snapped

Self Inflicted Tears

The tears that drown my vision
They are no longer for you
They haven't been in some time
Those tears I cry
Staring at my ceiling high
Those tears are for me
They weep for the person I was
The person I lost
The person who destroyed themselves
Destroyed for another person
Another person who is gone
Not gone from the world
But gone from my life
Absent here
Yet present in another story
Now again alone, I fear
But alone I'll find my own glory

Toxic

Sometimes caring too much is a bad thing
Sometimes I get stuck in my head
Sometimes I have conversations with you in my
sleep
Sometimes I hold on when you want to go
Sometimes I am too much
Sometimes I do too much
Sometimes I think too heavily with my feelings
Sometimes the good I intend becomes bad
Sometimes my help becomes stress
Sometimes questions get annoying
Sometimes my check ins get bothersome
Sometimes I am toxic
Both to you, and to myself
Yea, I'm toxic.

Tears

If I had a dollar for every tear I cried for you
I'd be a very rich man
But I'd still feel poor.
The wealth of a happy heart,
And a soul on fire,
Is beyond any worldly desire.

41 Days (2016)

The roof he was underneath
When he couldn't breathe
Get to the wedding was his mission
But he had a terrible condition
Doctor gave an answer
Said he had the lung cancer
Determined to survive
His will to win did thrive
But as if from a curse
It started to get worse
His left side was consumed
Doctors thought he was doomed
Yet he had the brawn
And he struggled on
For 40 long days
He didn't part ways
For 40 long nights
He fought under the lights
But on the 41st day
The hospital he wouldn't stay
Allowed to go home
To his house to roam
Not far into the living room
It became his tomb
The whole family was there

To give him a goodbye prayer

Now we all sit and pout
And wonder how his soul could let out
All I can do now is cry,
Because I couldn't say goodbye
I truly do have sorrow
Maybe I'll see you tomorrow...

But never again will a box come
That was labeled "from the GUM."

Never again will I have fun
With the one who called me "dog son."

And never again will I go on a hike
With my only Uncle Mike.

A Restless Night (2022)

A restless night,
the sky, black.
I look out and wonder
Is it spite?-
or payback?
Guess I'll look under-
those faux walls
where no one calls-
you true friends,
one who depends-
on you to be there,
always with care.
Always?
Always…
So many lies with that word.
It's truly absurd.
But what do I know?
I ought to go slow
It's just another mental brawl
And really after all,
It's nothing I can fight-
for, It's just a restless night.

My Place (2022)

It is said that days are long,
but the years are short.
So I write my song
as we sail from port.
With a proud note here
and a sad line there,
I sipe cheap beer-
and feel salt air-
beat my face-
while I waste my day-
seeking my own place,
longing for a stay.
At some place?
Not at A place,
but at My Own place.
As I make my chase,
wishing an act of grace
would end my ceaseless roam
and safely guide me home.
Ah, if only I knew!
But this venture is a failing quiz,
as on this vast ocean blue,
I do not know, where home is…

Waves (2022)

If your life is a journey,
then mine is a voyage.
A former proud ship
now stranded alone.
Becalmed in an open sea
helpless without wind.
Going nowhere fast,
trekking without a heading.
Simply drifting with the tide.
Floating, wherever it might go
unable to steer clear or-
veer away from rocks so near.
These are troubled waters indeed.
Control, to the waves, you cede.

Heartbreak & Hennessy

Even after all these drinks
My mind never stops and thinks,
"If I'd stop pouring this liquor,
Maybe I'd get better quicker."

I honestly struggle to remember
The last time I was happy with life
Not even the 21st night of September
Could save me from my inner strife

See, this violent thing called love
That we so dearly dream of,
Finding our one and only
Often leaves us wrecked and lonely.

I'm sorry I couldn't give you space
You just made me feel alive
Then you threw my heart back in my face
And my will power took a dive

You told me you were crazy
It made my mind so hazy
You said to leave you alone
Like, why'd you even text my phone?

As for now
I sadly vow
I do not know
Where I will go

& I think, as I light this cigarette
"I really want emotional clemency.
I guess though that's what I get,
For mixing heartbreak & Hennessy."

Hero

I'm sure I'm nobody's hero
More than likely I'm your zero
But that's all okay
Because I'm here today
I'm not going away
And I'm happy to say
I didn't need you
Not to get me through
No, I just needed me.
Now I do feel more free
And I changed my behavior
Knowing I was my own savior
See, not all hero's wear capes
They also come in different shapes
And when I look in the mirror
It's now become clearer:
I'm my own biggest fan,
I'm my own Superman.

Hope

Enough is enough
It's time to get better
I don't care how tough
Got to be a go-getter!
So let's pick up our shoulders
Even though they're heavier when we're sad
Let's stop slouching forward
And let's Move them back in place
Let's lift up our heads
And stop staring at the ground
Let's stop looking down to mood
Rather, let's look up to the sky with hope
No longer will we mope
Today is our day
Just as tomorrow will be too.

So somehow, someway
Despite the lonely hours
You'll make the most of today
And you'll find your true powers

Wish You Were Here

What is it about happiness that scares me?
The smiling?
The love?
Is it that I don't believe in it?
Or maybe I'm not allowed to feel it?
No, no not that.
Perhaps, I'm just a negative little shit?
I agreed with myself while at the beach, I sat.
About then, the cool of the wind had hit.
Oh, how the waves they crashed
but for me, I was trashed.
The brews I had brought,
what a good fucking thought.
They sure warmed me up!
Now a plenty empty cup
saw me feelin' the booze
so I started to write
from my mind thoughts ooze
onto the paper-white.

My body is tired and cold,
my mind is just numb.
I'd sure like for someone to hold,
but it won't happen, I'm so dumb.

I stop for some time,
I give up the rhyme.
I open another beer,
and just wish you were here.

www.ingramcontent.com/pod-product-compliance
Lightning Source LLC
La Vergne TN
LVHW010838200726
843508LV00012B/2648